AMANPREET KAUR

The Ultimate Guide to Making Money Online

How to Earn Money with Your Smartphone

Contents

Introduction

In today's fast-paced digital age, smartphones have become more than just communication devices; they are powerful tools for unlocking financial opportunities. "The Ultimate Guide to Making Money Online" is your essential companion on a journey to financial freedom. In this introduction, we set the stage for your exciting exploration of the world of mobile-based income generation.

1. The Digital Revolution: How Smartphones Have Changed the Game

The digital revolution has reshaped our lives in unprecedented ways, and at the forefront of this transformation stands the smartphone. These pocket-sized wonders have revolutionized the way we work, communicate, and even make money. In the first chapter, we delve deep into how smartphones have ushered in a new era of possibilities, allowing individuals from all walks of life to tap into previously unimaginable income streams. From the gig economy to online marketplaces, the smartphone has truly changed the game, and we'll show you how to play it to your advantage.

2. Understanding the Potential: Exploring the Versatility of

Your Smartphone

Your smartphone is a versatile Swiss army knife of modern living. Beyond just calls and text messages, it has an array of features and capabilities waiting to be harnessed for your financial benefit. In the second chapter, we take a closer look at your smartphone's potential and explore the many ways you can use it to generate income. From app-based platforms to e-commerce, content creation, and remote work, you'll gain insights into the vast spectrum of opportunities at your fingertips.

Get ready to unlock the full potential of your smartphone and embark on a journey towards financial empowerment. "The Ultimate Guide to Making Money Online" will guide you through every step of the way, providing valuable tips, strategies, and real-world examples to help you make the most of your digital tool. The world of online income is waiting for you, and it all starts with understanding the incredible potential of your smartphone.

Chapter 1: Leveraging the Power of Apps

1. Identifying Profitable App Categories:

In today's digital era mobile applications play a significant role in our daily lives. From social media and entertainment to productivity and finance there is an app for almost every aspect of our lives. As an aspiring app developer or someone looking to make money through apps it is essential to identify profitable app categories that have a high user demand and potential for generating revenue.

To identify profitable app categories you can conduct market research to understand current trends consumer preferences and areas where there might be gaps or opportunities for improvement. For example if you notice that there is a growing interest in health and fitness developing an app that offers workout routines nutrition plans and progress tracking might be a profitable venture.

Additionally you can analyze the top-grossing apps in app stores like the Apple App Store and Google Play Store. These platforms provide rankings based on revenue generated by each app category giving you insights into the most profitable areas.

Keep in mind that the app market is vast and there is competition in every category. To stand out and succeed you should consider offering unique features a great user experience and adding value to the users' lives.

2. Developing Your Own App for Passive Income:

Developing your own app can be an excellent way to generate passive income. However it requires proper planning execution and ongoing maintenance. Here are the key steps involved in developing an app for passive income:

a. Idea Generation: Start by brainstorming app ideas that align with your interests skills and market demands. Consider the profitable app categories you identified earlier and think about how you can create an app that meets users' needs or addresses their pain points.

b. Research and Planning: Conduct thorough market research to validate your app idea and identify potential competitors. This research will help you understand your target audience their expectations and the features that will make your app unique. Create a detailed plan that outlines your app's functionalities user interface and development timeline.

c. Design and Development: Once you have a solid plan begin designing the user interface and experience for your app. You can either hire a professional app design and development team or learn to code yourself if you have the necessary skills. It is crucial to create a visually appealing user-friendly and smooth-functioning app.

d. Testing and Refinement: Before launching your app conduct extensive testing to identify and fix any bugs or issues. Enlist a group of beta testers who can provide valuable feedback about the app's performance usability and overall experience. Use their feedback to refine and improve your app further.

e. Launch and Marketing: When your app is ready publish it on the relevant app stores and create a marketing strategy to promote it. Leverage digital marketing techniques such as search engine optimization (SEO social media marketing and influencer collaborations to increase your app's visibility and attract potential users.

f. Monetization: To generate passive income consider various monetization strategies for your app such as in-app advertisements paid premium features subscription models or affiliate partnerships. Choose a monetization model that suits your app and target audience while also ensuring a sustainable revenue stream.

g. Ongoing Maintenance and Updates: Once your app is live it requires regular maintenance and updates to keep it running smoothly and retain user engagement. Analyze user feedback app analytics and market trends to identify areas of improvement and implement updates accordingly.

3. Monetizing Existing Apps through Ads and In-App Purchases:

If you already have an app but haven't monetized it yet there are multiple ways you can generate income from your existing user base. Two popular methods are through in-app advertisements and in-app purchases.

a. In-App Advertisements: Advertising can be a lucrative way to monetize your app. You can display ads within your app either through banner ads interstitial ads (full-screen ads that appear between app screens or video ads. These ads can be sourced from ad networks like Google AdMob Facebook Audience Network or direct partnerships with advertisers.

It is crucial to strike a balance between monetization and user experience. Intrusive or excessive ads may lead to user dissatisfaction and decreased engagement. Ensure that the ads are relevant to the app's niche non-obtrusive and easy to dismiss for a better user experience.

b. In-App Purchases: In-app purchases enable users to unlock additional features content or virtual goods within the app for a fee. This model is commonly used in gaming apps where users can purchase virtual items power-ups or character upgrades.

To successfully monetize through in-app purchases design your app in a way that offers a compelling and engaging experience for free while providing users with desirable premium content or features through purchases. Make sure the pricing is reasonable and the value offered justifies the cost to increase the likelihood of purchases.

4. Exploring App Testing and Beta Programs:

App testing and beta programs are essential steps in the app development process to ensure that your app is bug-free user-friendly and meets the expectations of your target audience. Here's what you need to know about app testing and beta programs:

a. Alpha Testing: Alpha testing is the initial phase of testing where you test your app within your development team or a small group of trusted individuals. This process helps identify and fix any major issues or functionality gaps before moving to the next stage.

b. Beta Testing: Beta testing involves releasing an unfinished version of your app to a wider group of testers who represent your target audience. These testers provide valuable feedback on the app's usability performance and overall experience. Their feedback can help you make necessary improvements and identify any remaining bugs or issues.

c. Beta Programs: Many app stores including the Apple App Store and the Google Play Store offer beta testing programs where developers can enroll their apps and invite a broader group of beta testers. This allows you to gather feedback at scale and address any issues before the final app release.

d. User Feedback: During the testing and beta phase encourage testers to provide feedback through surveys bug reports or in-app feedback mechanisms. Analyze this feedback and prioritize necessary changes or improvements based on its relevance and impact on the app's usability and user experience.

e. Continuous Testing: Even after the initial release ongoing testing and updates are crucial to maintain your app's quality and performance. Regularly monitor user feedback review app analytics and stay updated with the latest devices and operating system versions to ensure compatibility and optimal performance.

In conclusion leveraging the power of apps can be a lucrative way to make money online. By identifying profitable app categories developing your own app monetizing existing apps and implementing comprehensive testing and beta programs you can maximize your chances of success in the ever-growing app market.

Chapter 2: Unlocking the World of E-Commerce

1. Building a Profitable E-Commerce Business on Your Smartphone

In today's digital age smartphones play a crucial role in enabling individuals to start and run profitable e-commerce businesses. With the right tools and strategies you can leverage your mobile device to make money from anywhere in the world. Here we will delve into various avenues for generating income through e-commerce on your smartphone.

One of the most effective ways to earn money with your mobile phone is by establishing your own e-commerce business. With the rise of user-friendly e-commerce platforms and apps setting up an online store has become easier than ever. You can choose to sell physical products digital products or even services. This chapter will focus on selling physical products through online marketplaces like Amazon eBay and Etsy as well as utilizing dropshipping and print-on-demand business models.

2. Selling Physical Products through Online Marketplaces

Online marketplaces provide an excellent platform for selling physical products without the need to invest heavily in inventory or manage shipping and fulfillment processes. Platforms like Amazon eBay and Etsy offer millions of potential customers and provide a user-friendly interface to list and manage your products.

To get started you need to research trending product categories identify products with low competition and high demand and source them from reliable suppliers. You can use tools like Jungle Scout or Helium 10 to conduct product research and find profitable niches.

Once you've identified the products you want to sell you can create compelling product listings using high-quality images and well-written descriptions. Effective product branding and packaging can help differentiate your products and attract customers.

To optimize your sales you should also leverage the power of reviews and ratings. Encourage satisfied customers to leave feedback and monitor and address any negative reviews promptly. Continuously improving your product quality and customer experience will lead to better ratings positioning your products higher in search results and driving more sales.

3. Dropshipping and Print-On-Demand: Maximizing Profit Margins

Dropshipping and print-on-demand (POD) are two popular e-commerce models that allow you to earn money without the need for upfront inventory investments. These business models eliminate the hassle of managing stock shipping and fulfillment making them ideal for mobile entrepreneurs.

Dropshipping involves partnering with suppliers who handle inventory and fulfillment on your behalf. When a customer places an order on your online store you forward the order details to the supplier who then ships the product directly to the customer. Your profit comes from the difference between the wholesale price and the retail price you set.

Print-on-demand allows you to sell customized products such as t-shirts mugs phone cases and more. Once a customer places an order the POD company prints the design on the product and ships it directly to the customer. With POD you can create unique designs target specific niches and earn passive income.

To excel in dropshipping and print-on-demand you should focus on finding reliable suppliers with high-quality products competitive pricing and efficient shipping. Building a strong brand and marketing your products effectively are also key to attracting customers and driving sales.

4. Growing and Managing Your Online Store with Smartphone Tools

Running a successful e-commerce business requires effective management and growth strategies. Fortunately mobile apps and tools can help you streamline operations and scale your business.

Marketplace seller apps like Amazon Seller Central and eBay Seller Hub enable you to manage your listings monitor sales and communicate with customers from your smartphone. These apps provide real-time analytics and insights to help optimize your selling strategy.

Social media platforms like Instagram and Facebook offer powerful marketing tools to promote your products and engage with your target audience. You can create targeted ads collaborate with influencers and build a loyal customer base through engaging content and effective social media marketing strategies.

Tools like Canva and Adobe Spark allow you to create captivating visuals and graphics for your product listings social media posts and advertisements. These apps provide user-friendly templates and editing tools to enhance your brand presence and attract customers.

Mobile payment solutions like PayPal Stripe and Square enable you to accept payments securely and conveniently. These platforms integrate seamlessly with e-commerce platforms and provide instant payment processing which boosts customer trust and enhances the shopping experience.

In conclusion the opportunities to earn money through e-commerce on a smartphone are endless. By leveraging online marketplaces utilizing dropshipping and print-on-demand models and using smartphone tools for business management and growth you can build a profitable e-commerce business from the comfort of your handheld device. With dedication research and continuous improvement your smartphone can become a powerful tool for generating income in the world of e-commerce.

Chapter 3: Content Creation and Monetization

1. Becoming a Social Media Influencer: Strategies for Success

In today's digital age social media has become a powerful platform for individuals to share their thoughts experiences and expertise with the world. Becoming a social media influencer allows you to leverage your online presence and build a loyal following. Here are some strategies for success:

a. Identify your niche: To stand out in the crowded social media landscape it's crucial to find your niche. Determine what topics you're passionate about and where your expertise lies. This will help you target a specific audience and establish yourself as an authority in that field.

b. Create high-quality content: Consistently create compelling content that resonates with your audience. Whether it's through photos videos or written posts focus on providing value entertainment or inspiration. Use professional equipment and editing tools to ensure the quality is top-notch.

c. Engage with your audience: Building a strong connection

with your audience is essential. Respond to comments answer questions and engage in meaningful conversations. Show genuine interest in your followers and build a community around your content.

d. Collaborate with other influencers: Collaborating with other influencers can help you expand your reach and gain exposure to new audiences. Look for influencers in complimentary niches and explore opportunities for joint content creation or cross-promotion.

e. Build your personal brand: Establish a distinct brand identity that reflects your personality values and style. Consistency is key in building brand recognition. Use a consistent visual aesthetic tone of voice and storytelling approach across all your social media platforms.

f. Partner with brands: As your following grows you'll have the opportunity to collaborate with brands for sponsored content. Partnerships can range from product reviews to sponsored posts and even brand ambassadorships. Choose brands that align with your values and resonate with your audience.

g. Diversify your income streams: Beyond brand collaborations consider diversifying your income streams. This can include selling digital products offering online courses or coaching or leveraging affiliate marketing.

2. Creating Engaging and Profitable YouTube Channels

YouTube has revolutionized the way we consume video content

and it has also become a lucrative platform for content creators. Here are some steps to create engaging and profitable YouTube channels:

a. Identify your niche and target audience: Determine the type of content you want to create and who your target audience is. Think about what unique value you can offer to stand out in the vast YouTube landscape.

b. Create high-quality videos: Invest in good equipment including a high-resolution camera good lighting and clear audio. Make sure your videos are well-edited and visually appealing. Keep them engaging and informative and always strive to deliver value to your viewers.

c. Optimize your videos for search: YouTube is a search engine so optimizing your videos for discoverability is crucial. Use relevant keywords in your title description and tags. Craft compelling thumbnails and write detailed video descriptions to help users find your content.

d. Build a loyal subscriber base: Encourage viewers to subscribe to your channel by consistently delivering valuable content. Engage with your audience through comments and video responses. Regularly ask for feedback and suggestions to foster a sense of community.

e. Monetize your YouTube channel: Once you've built a substantial subscriber base and have met YouTube's monetization requirements you'll be able to monetize your channel. This can be done through ads sponsored content merchandise sales or membership programs.

f. Utilize YouTube's features: Take advantage of YouTube's features to engage and retain your audience. Encourage user interactions by enabling comments likes and shares. Use end screens and annotations to promote other relevant videos or channels. Additionally use YouTube's analytics to gain insights into your audience's behavior and preferences.

g. Collaborate with other YouTubers: Collaborating with other YouTubers can help you tap into new audiences and grow your channel faster. Seek out creators with similar interests or complementary content and explore collaboration opportunities such as guest appearances or content swaps.

3. Starting a Podcast and Generating Revenue

Podcasting has exploded in popularity providing individuals with a unique platform to share their ideas stories and expertise. Here's a guide to starting a podcast and generating revenue from it:

a. Identify your podcast niche and target audience: Determine the focus of your podcast and who your target audience is. This will help you tailor your content and attract a loyal listenership.

b. Plan your episodes: Create a content plan or outline for each episode ensuring that it provides value insights or entertainment to your audience. Consider using a consistent format or theme to establish a sense of familiarity.

c. Invest in good audio equipment: Clear audio quality is vital for a successful podcast. Invest in a good microphone and audio editing software to ensure your episodes sound professional. Minimize background noise and optimize the audio levels for a pleasant listening experience.

d. Publish and promote your podcast: Choose a reliable podcast hosting platform to publish and distribute your episodes to various podcast directories. Promote your podcast on social media platforms your website and other relevant channels to expand your listener base.

e. Engage with your listeners: Encourage listener feedback by inviting them to share their thoughts questions or suggestions. Respond to comments and messages promptly and incorporate listener insights into future episodes. Building a community around your podcast will help foster loyalty and engagement.

f. Monetize your podcast: There are several ways to monetize a podcast. Some common strategies include advertising sponsorships crowdfunding merchandise sales or offering premium content or bonus episodes to paid subscribers. Explore partnerships with relevant brands or consider creating your own products or services related to your podcast's niche.

g. Leverage other platforms: Use your podcast as a springboard to establish a presence on other platforms. Cross-promote your podcast on social media create blog posts or articles based on your podcast episodes or record video versions of your podcast for YouTube or other video-sharing platforms.

4. Blogging: Turning Your Passion into Profit

Blogging is a versatile and accessible platform for sharing your knowledge experiences and passions with a global audience. Here's a step-by-step guide to turning your blog into a profitable venture:

a. Choose your niche and target audience: Determine the focus of your blog and who your target audience is. Narrowing down your niche will help you create content that resonates with a specific audience.

b. Set up your blog: Choose a reliable blogging platform such as WordPress or Blogger and set up your blog. Purchase a domain name that reflects your blog's branding and ensure your website design is user-friendly and visually appealing.

c. Create valuable and engaging content: Consistently create high-quality content that provides value insights or entertainment to your audience. Use a mix of text images and multimedia to make your content visually appealing and engaging. Incorporate keywords strategically to improve your blog's search engine rankings.

d. Build a loyal readership: Engage with your readers by responding to comments starting discussions and encouraging feedback. Regularly promote your blog on social media channels email newsletters or relevant forums to attract a wider audience. Offer incentives such as free downloadable resources or exclusive content to encourage readers to subscribe to your mailing list.

e. Monetize your blog: There are various ways to monetize a blog. These include display advertising sponsored content affiliate marketing selling digital products or courses offering consulting or coaching services or even publishing a book based on your blog's content. Choose monetization methods that align with your blog's niche and audience.

f. Develop your personal brand: Build a personal brand around your blog by creating a consistent visual identity using a distinct tone of voice and establishing yourself as an expert in your niche. Collaborate with other bloggers or influencers be a guest contributor on other websites or publications and network with industry professionals to increase your visibility and credibility.

g. Analyze and optimize: Continuously analyze your blog's performance using analytics tools. Pay attention to metrics such as page views engagement rates and conversion rates for your monetization efforts. Use this data to optimize your content strategy improve user experience and fine-tune your monetization tactics.

In conclusion creating and monetizing content requires a strategic approach consistency and a deep understanding of your target audience. Whether you choose to become a social media influencer start a YouTube channel launch a podcast or run a blog following these strategies and continuously adapting to the ever-evolving digital landscape will help you turn your passion into profit.

Chapter 4: Freelancing and Remote Work Opportunities

1. Finding Freelance Gigs and Job Platforms

In today's digital world opportunities for freelancers and remote workers abound. Whether you're a writer graphic designer translator or possess any other marketable skills your smartphone can be a powerful tool to tap into the gig economy. Here are some ways to leverage your smartphone to find freelance gigs and job platforms:

a) Freelance job platforms: There are numerous platforms dedicated to connecting freelancers with job opportunities. Examples include Upwork Freelancer Fiverr and Guru. These platforms often have dedicated mobile apps that allow you to create profiles browse job listings communicate with clients and even complete projects directly from your smartphone.

b) Social media platforms: Social media can be a valuable tool for finding freelance gigs. Platforms like LinkedIn Facebook groups and Twitter can help you connect with potential clients in your desired industry. By showcasing your skills sharing relevant content and actively engaging with others you can increase your visibility and attract potential work opportunities.

c) Freelance marketplaces: Alongside job platforms there are various online marketplaces tailored specifically for freelancers. For writers platforms like Constant Content Textbroker and WriterAccess offer writing gigs. Designers can utilize platforms like 99designs or DesignCrowd to find graphic design projects. These platforms often have mobile apps that allow you to manage your projects communicate with clients and deliver your work.

2. Offering Digital Services: Writing Graphic Design Translation and More

Once you've connected with clients or identified potential opportunities your smartphone can help you offer your digital services efficiently. Here are some examples of how you can leverage your smartphone to deliver high-quality work:

a) Writing: With writing apps like Google Docs Microsoft Word or even specialized writing tools like Scrivener you can craft content collaborate with clients and track changes all from your smartphone. Communication and file-sharing apps like Slack and Dropbox can also streamline the review and feedback process with your clients.

b) Graphic design: Various graphic design apps on smartphones such as Adobe Spark Canva or Over offer powerful tools for creating visual content. These apps are designed to work seamlessly on mobile devices enabling you to design logos social media graphics or marketing materials on the go.

c) Translation: If you're skilled in multiple languages your smartphone can open up doors for translation work. Tools like Google Translate Microsoft Translator or dedicated translation apps can help you communicate with clients in different languages and efficiently translate documents or content.

d) Online tutoring: If you have expertise in a particular subject you can offer online tutoring services through your smartphone. Apps like Zoom Skype or Google Meet allow you to conduct virtual tutoring sessions share educational materials and communicate with students remotely.

3. Remote Work: Embracing the Digital Nomad Lifestyle

Beyond freelancing remote work is a growing trend that offers flexibility and freedom to professionals. The rise of smartphones has made it easier to work remotely from anywhere in the world. Here's how you can embrace the digital nomad lifestyle:

a) Virtual meetings and collaboration: Communication tools like Zoom Slack or Microsoft Teams enable remote workers to participate in virtual meetings and collaborate with colleagues seamlessly. These apps can be accessed on smartphones making it easier to stay connected while working remotely.

b) Cloud storage and file sharing: Services like Google Drive Dropbox or Microsoft OneDrive allow you to store and access your work files from anywhere. With a smartphone you can upload or download files collaborate on documents and share files with colleagues eliminating the need for physical storage devices.

c) Project management tools: Remote work often involves managing projects and tasks. Smartphone-compatible project management tools like Trello Asana or Monday.com help you stay organized track progress and collaborate with team members even when you're on the move.

d) Time management and productivity: Productivity apps like Todoist Evernote or Forest can help you manage your tasks set reminders and block distractions. With the help of these apps you can stay focused and maximize your productivity regardless of your location.

4. Managing Finances Contracts and Client Relationships on Your Smartphone

Managing your freelancing or remote work business doesn't stop with delivering projects. It's essential to handle finances contracts and client relationships effectively. Here are some ways your smartphone can assist in these areas:

a) Invoicing and payment apps: Many invoicing apps such as FreshBooks Wave or QuickBooks offer mobile versions that allow you to create and send professional invoices track payments and even accept payments directly through your smartphone. This helps streamline your financial management process.

b) Contract management tools: Apps like HelloSign DocuSign or Adobe Sign enable you to sign send and manage contracts digitally. You can review contracts add electronic signatures and send them to clients for immediate approval all from your smartphone.

c) Customer relationship management (CRM) apps: Maintaining strong client relationships is crucial for continued business success. CRM tools like HubSpot Salesforce or Zoho CRM provide mobile apps that allow you to manage client interactions track communication history and stay organized while on the move.

d) Communication and networking: As a freelancer or remote worker communication is key. Apps like Skype Slack or WhatsApp make it easy to stay in touch with clients colleagues and industry contacts whether through messaging voice calls or video conferences. Networking on professional platforms like LinkedIn can also help you expand your client base and stay connected with potential work opportunities.

In conclusion smartphones have become an indispensable tool for freelancers and remote workers offering a wide range of opportunities to find gigs offer digital services work remotely and manage business operations. By harnessing the power and flexibility of smartphones you can enhance your productivity work from anywhere and thrive in today's digital economy.

Chapter 5: Investing Strategies for the Modern Entrepreneur

1. Introduction to Mobile Investing Apps

In the modern era entrepreneurs have access to a plethora of tools that can help them manage their investments conveniently and efficiently. The rise of mobile investing apps has made it possible for entrepreneurs to monitor and make investment decisions on the go without relying on traditional methods or personal financial advisors.

Mobile investing apps come in various forms offering features such as real-time stock quotes customizable watchlists portfolio tracking and even the ability to execute trades directly from the app. These apps provide entrepreneurs with access to financial markets at their fingertips allowing them to stay updated on market trends and make informed investment decisions at any time.

One popular mobile investing app is Robinhood. Robinhood offers commission-free trading on stocks ETFs options and cryptocurrencies. It provides real-time market data and allows users to create watchlists and trade directly from their smartphones. Another popular app is Acorns which allows users to invest their spare change by rounding up their purchases to the nearest dollar and investing the difference.

2. Building a Diverse Investment Portfolio on Your Smartphone

Diversification is a key component of any successful investment strategy. It involves spreading investments across different asset classes industries and geographies to reduce risk and maximize potential returns. Mobile investing apps make it easier than ever for entrepreneurs to build and maintain a diverse investment portfolio.

Mobile investing apps offer a wide range of investment options including stocks bonds mutual funds ETFs and even alternative investments such as cryptocurrencies. Entrepreneurs can use these apps to research and invest in different asset classes based on their risk tolerance and investment objectives.

For example an entrepreneur could use a mobile investing app to invest in a mix of stocks from various industries bonds for fixed income and ETFs to gain exposure to specific sectors or regions. By diversifying their investments entrepreneurs can reduce the impact of any single investment's performance on their overall portfolio.

3. Exploring Cryptocurrency and Blockchain Opportunities

Cryptocurrencies and blockchain technology have gained significant attention in recent years. These emerging technologies have the potential to disrupt traditional industries and create new investment opportunities for entrepreneurs. Mobile investing apps allow entrepreneurs to explore and invest in cryptocurrencies and blockchain-related assets conveniently.

Apps like Coinbase and Binance offer a user-friendly interface for buying selling and storing cryptocurrencies. Entrepreneurs can use these apps to invest in popular cryptocurrencies like Bitcoin and Ethereum as well as explore new blockchain projects through initial coin offerings (ICOs) and decentralized finance (DeFi) platforms.

Investing in cryptocurrencies carries unique risks due to their volatility and regulatory uncertainty. However for entrepreneurs who understand and are willing to tolerate these risks mobile investing apps provide a convenient way to participate in the cryptocurrency market and potentially benefit from its growth.

4. Tracking and Analyzing Investment Performance on the Go

Monitoring the performance of investments is crucial for entrepreneurs to evaluate the success of their strategies and make informed decisions. Mobile investing apps offer comprehensive tools for tracking and analyzing investment performance allowing entrepreneurs to stay on top of their financial goals.

Mobile investing apps provide real-time updates on the value and performance of investments enabling entrepreneurs to track their portfolio's performance at any time. These apps often offer interactive charts and graphs allowing users to visualize their investment returns over different time periods and compare them to benchmarks or indices.

Furthermore mobile investing apps often provide sophisticated analytics tools that allow entrepreneurs to assess the risk and performance of their investments. These tools may include features such as portfolio analysis asset allocation analysis and risk assessment based on historical data and statistical models.

By leveraging the tracking and analysis tools offered by mobile investing apps entrepreneurs can gain valuable insights into their investment performance and make adjustments to their strategies as needed.

5. Utilizing Robo-Advisors for Automated Investing

Robo-advisors have become increasingly popular among modern entrepreneurs due to their convenience and cost-effectiveness. These digital platforms use algorithms to automate investment decisions based on your goals risk tolerance and time horizon. With just a few taps on your smartphone you can set up an account with a robo-advisor and start investing.

One popular robo-advisor is Betterment. It offers a range of investment options that are diversified across various asset classes such as stocks bonds and real estate. When you sign up for Betterment you'll answer a series of questions to determine your financial goals and risk tolerance. The platform then creates a personalized investment portfolio for you and automatically rebalances it as needed.

For example let's say you have a moderate risk tolerance and a goal of saving for retirement. Betterment might allocate a higher percentage of your portfolio to stocks for potential long-term growth and a smaller percentage to bonds for stability. As you get closer to retirement the platform will adjust the allocation to reduce risk and preserve your wealth.

Another popular robo-advisor is Wealthfront. It uses a similar algorithmic approach to create and manage portfolios for its users. Wealthfront also offers additional features like tax-loss harvesting which can help minimize your taxable gains.

By using robo-advisors modern entrepreneurs can benefit from professional investment management at a fraction of the cost charged by traditional financial advisors. These platforms are accessible through mobile apps allowing you to monitor your investments and make adjustments whenever and wherever you want.

6. Exploring Social Trading Platforms for Collaborative Investing

Social trading platforms have revolutionized the way investors interact and learn from each other. Through these platforms you can connect with a community of traders follow their investment strategies and even copy their trades automatically.

One prominent social trading platform is eToro. It allows users to browse and follow the portfolio of successful traders evaluate their performance and decide whether to replicate their trades. This approach is particularly beneficial for modern entrepreneurs who may not have extensive knowledge or experience in investing but still want to participate in the market.

Imagine you come across a highly successful trader on eToro who consistently generates impressive returns. You can choose to allocate a portion of your investment capital to automatically copy their trades. This way you can benefit from their expertise while learning and gaining confidence in your own investment decisions.

Social trading platforms facilitate collaboration and knowledge sharing among investors empowering even novice entrepreneurs to make informed investment choices. Accessible through mobile apps these platforms enable real-time interactions and allow you to stay connected with the trading community wherever you go.

7. Leveraging Trading Apps for Active Investing

While robo-advisors and social trading platforms are well-suited for passive or semi-passive investing active entrepreneurs may prefer to take a more hands-on approach. Trading apps such as TD Ameritrade's thinkorswim or Robinhood cater to these individuals by providing powerful tools and real-time market data for making active investment decisions.

For example thinkorswim offers advanced charting capabilities and technical analysis tools that allow you to analyze price movements identify trends and make informed trading decisions. The app also provides access to news and research reports keeping you informed about market developments that could impact your investments.

Robinhood on the other hand prides itself on its commission-free trades making it an attractive option for cost-conscious entrepreneurs. The app's user-friendly interface and simplified trading experience make it easy for beginners to start trading stocks options and cryptocurrencies directly from their smartphones.

Modern entrepreneurs can leverage these trading apps to actively manage their investment portfolios and take advantage of short-term market opportunities. However it's important to note that active trading comes with higher risks and requires more time and effort for research and monitoring.

8. Considering Alternative Investment Opportunities

In addition to traditional asset classes like stocks and bonds modern entrepreneurs can use their smartphones to explore alternative investment opportunities such as real estate crowdfunding peer-to-peer lending and even art or collectible investments.

Real estate crowdfunding platforms like Fundrise and Realty-Mogul allow individuals to invest in real estate projects with relatively small amounts of capital. These platforms connect investors with developers seeking funding for residential or commercial properties. Through mobile apps entrepreneurs can review property information financial projections and historical returns to make informed investment decisions.

Peer-to-peer lending platforms like Prosper and LendingClub provide an alternative to traditional banking institutions by connecting borrowers directly with individual investors. Using these apps entrepreneurs can lend money to individuals or small businesses and earn interest on their investments. The platforms handle the loan origination servicing and collection processes making it easy for investors to diversify their portfolios across multiple loans.

Art and collectibles have also become accessible investment classes through platforms like Masterworks and Rally. These apps allow investors to buy shares in valuable artworks collectible cars rare trading cards and other high-end assets. By fractionalizing ownership entrepreneurs can invest in these passion-driven assets at a fraction of the cost potentially earning returns as the value of the asset appreciates over time.

By considering alternative investment opportunities modern entrepreneurs can further diversify their portfolios and potentially earn attractive returns outside of traditional asset classes. The convenience of mobile apps makes it easier than ever to explore research and invest in these alternative options.

9. Mitigating Risks and Staying Informed

While investing through smartphone apps offers convenience and flexibility it's crucial for modern entrepreneurs to understand the risks involved and take necessary precautions to protect their investments. Here are a few key considerations:

a. Security: Ensure that the mobile investing apps you use have robust security measures in place such as two-factor authentication and data encryption. Regularly update your app and smartphone to install the latest security patches.

b. Research and Due Diligence: Before making any investment decisions thoroughly research and evaluate the investment opportunities available through mobile apps. Consider the track record fees and transparency of the investment platform or service provider.

c. Diversification: Spread your investments across different asset classes and geographical regions to reduce the impact of any single investment's performance on your overall portfolio.

d. Risk Tolerance: Understand and assess your risk tolerance to ensure that the investment strategies you employ through mobile apps align with your comfort level. Avoid making impulsive decisions based on short-term market fluctuations.

e. Continuous Learning: Stay informed by following investment news subscribing to market newsletters and joining online communities or forums related to investing. Maintain a learning mindset and adapt your investment strategies as needed.

Conclusion

Mobile investing apps have revolutionized the way modern entrepreneurs access and manage their investments. From robo-advisors for automated investing to social trading platforms for collaborative investing and trading apps for active investing there are a plethora of options available at your fingertips. Additionally alternative investment opportunities allow entrepreneurs to diversify their portfolios beyond traditional assets. However it is important to mitigate risks by practicing due diligence diversifying investments and staying informed about market trends. With the right strategies and tools mobile investing apps can empower entrepreneurs to successfully navigate the world of investing.

Chapter 6: Maximizing Savings and Cashback Opportunities

1. Cashback Apps: Getting Paid for Everyday Purchases

Cashback apps are a popular way to earn money while shopping for everyday items. These apps offer cashback or rewards for making purchases through their platforms or by scanning your receipts. Here's how they work:

Example: **Ibotta** is a cashback app that offers rebates on grocery store purchases. Users can browse offers on the app, buy eligible items, and then take a picture of their receipt. They receive cashback in their Ibotta account, which they can later transfer to their bank account or use for gift cards.

2. Couponing and Discount Aggregators: Unlocking Savings

Couponing and discount aggregator platforms help you find and use coupons, promo codes, and discounts to save money on various purchases, both online and offline. These services collect and curate deals from a wide range of retailers.

Example: **RetailMeNot** is a popular coupon and discount aggregator website. Users can search for deals and coupons for specific stores or products. When making an online purchase, they can apply the coupon codes they find on RetailMeNot during checkout to get discounts or free shipping.

3. Mobile Banking and Budgeting Tools: Managing Finances Efficiently

Mobile banking apps and budgeting tools are essential for managing your finances efficiently. They help you track your income, expenses, and savings goals, providing insights into your financial health.

Example: **Mint** is a comprehensive budgeting app that connects to your bank accounts, credit cards, and investments. It automatically categorizes your transactions, creates budgets, and provides financial insights to help you manage your money effectively.

4. Personal Finance and Investment Apps: Growing Your Wealth

Personal finance and investment apps empower you to make informed decisions about your money and investments. These apps offer tools and information to help you build wealth over time.

Example: **Robinhood** is a popular investment app that allows users to buy and sell stocks, ETFs, cryptocurrencies, and other assets with no trading commissions. It provides real-time market data and financial news to help users make informed investment choices.

By incorporating these strategies and tools into your financial routine, you can increase your savings, find discounts on your purchases, manage your finances more efficiently, and even grow your wealth over time. Each of these methods can contribute to a more secure and prosperous financial future.

5. Credit Card Rewards Programs: Maximizing Benefits

Credit card rewards programs offer a great way to earn cashback points or airline miles when making purchases using specific credit cards. These rewards can be accrued over time and redeemed for various benefits such as cashback travel rewards gift cards or merchandise.

There are different types of credit card rewards programs including cashback cards travel rewards cards and general rewards cards. Depending on your preferences and spending habits you can choose a credit card that aligns with your goals and offers the best rewards for your regular spending categories.

For example if you frequently travel a travel rewards card might be ideal as it offers benefits like airline miles and hotel discounts. If you prefer cashback look for a credit card that offers higher cashback percentages on everyday purchases like groceries or gas.

To maximize your savings and cashback opportunities with credit card rewards programs consider the following strategies:

a. Choose cards strategically: Research different credit cards and select those that offer rewards in categories where you spend the most. For instance if you spend significantly on dining and entertainment select a card that provides high cashback percentages or bonus points in these categories.

b. Pay attention to sign-up bonuses: Many credit cards offer sign-up bonuses as an incentive to new cardholders. These bonuses usually come with specific spending requirements within a certain time frame such as spending a certain amount in the first three months. By meeting these requirements you can earn a substantial amount of cashback or reward points upfront.

c. Use credit cards for everyday expenses: By using your rewards credit card for everyday expenses you can earn rewards on purchases that you would typically make anyway. However it's crucial to practice responsible credit card usage and pay off your balance in full each month to avoid interest charges.

d. Combine rewards: Some credit card rewards programs allow you to combine points or cashback from different cards or partner programs. This can be advantageous if you have multiple credit cards or if your chosen credit card offers the option to transfer points to partner loyalty programs. By consolidating your rewards you can often redeem them for more significant discounts or travel benefits.

e. Redeem wisely: When it comes to redeeming your rewards aim for maximizing their value. For example if your credit card offers a redemption option to convert points into cashback or statement credits this can be a valuable way to reduce your overall expenses. Similarly redeeming points for travel rewards like flights or hotel stays can provide significant savings.

Keep in mind that credit card rewards programs typically come with terms and conditions including annual fees interest rates and minimum spending requirements. Before applying for a credit card carefully review these terms to ensure the rewards outweigh any associated costs.

6. Cashback Websites and Browser Extensions: Extra Savings Online

Cashback websites and browser extensions offer consumers the opportunity to earn cashback or receive discounts when shopping online. These platforms partner with various retailers and earn a commission for referring customers to their websites. In turn they share a portion of that commission with the consumer in the form of cashback or rewards.

To take advantage of these opportunities follow these steps:

a. Sign up for cashback websites: There are several popular cashback websites such as Rakuten (formerly known as Ebates Swagbucks and TopCashback. Create an account on these platforms and explore their partnered retailers.

b. Activate browser extensions: Install browser extensions like Honey or RetailMeNot Genie which automatically notify you if there are any available cashback or discount offers when browsing through partner websites. These extensions help ensure you never miss out on potential savings.

c. Start shopping: When shopping online visit your preferred cashback website or use the browser extension to access a specific retailer. By doing so your purchases will be tracked and you will earn cashback or receive discounts based on the agreed-upon terms.

d. Cash out your earnings: Once your cashback accumulates to a certain threshold typically $20 or more you can request to withdraw your earnings. Depending on the platform you may have various options such as receiving a check gift cards or transferring the cashback to your PayPal account.

Keep in mind that cashback percentages vary by retailer and can range from 1% to 20% or more. It's advisable to compare rates across different cashback websites and browser extensions to ensure you're getting the best deal.

7. Loyalty and Membership Programs: Unlocking Additional Savings

Many retailers airlines hotels and other businesses offer loyalty and membership programs that provide exclusive discounts rewards and perks to their customers. By participating in these programs you can maximize your savings and cashback opportunities.

Here are some common loyalty and membership programs worth considering:

a. Retailer loyalty programs: Popular retailers like Target Wal-mart and Sephora offer loyalty programs that provide benefits like exclusive discounts personalized offers and early access to sales events. These programs often track your purchases and provide rewards in the form of store credit or cashback.

b. Airlines and hotels loyalty programs: If you frequently fly or stay at hotels joining loyalty programs offered by airlines and hotel chains can be highly beneficial. These programs often provide opportunities to earn miles or points for flights or stays which can be redeemed for free flights hotel stays upgrades or other travel-related benefits.

c. Grocery store loyalty programs: Many grocery store chains have loyalty programs that allow customers to earn points or cashback based on their purchases. These programs often offer special discounts on specific products or personalized coupons based on your shopping habits.

d. Membership clubs: Warehouse retailers like Costco or Sam's Club offer membership programs that provide access to discounted prices on a wide range of products. Additionally membership clubs often offer cashback rewards or special discounts on select items.

By signing up for loyalty and membership programs you can take advantage of these exclusive benefits and significantly increase your savings and cashback opportunities.

Conclusion

Maximizing savings and cashback opportunities is essential for efficient personal finance management. By utilizing various tools and strategies such as cashback apps couponing budgeting tools personal finance and investment apps credit card rewards programs cashback websites and browser extensions and loyalty and membership programs individuals can make the most of their spending and earn money back or receive discounts on their everyday purchases.

It's crucial to research and carefully analyze each opportunity to ensure it aligns with your financial goals and preferences. Additionally stay mindful of any associated fees terms and conditions and make sure to practice responsible spending habits to maximize your savings effectively.

Chapter 7: Opportunities in the Gig Economy

The gig economy has revolutionized the way people earn income by providing them with flexible work opportunities. With the rise of smartphones it has become even easier to access and participate in the gig economy. In this chapter we will explore four popular gig economy sectors where individuals can earn money using their smartphones: ride-sharing services food delivery task-based gig platforms and home rental services.

1. Ride-Sharing Services: Driving for Profit

Ride-sharing services like Uber Lyft and Grab have gained massive popularity across the globe. These platforms allow individuals to use their own vehicles to provide transportation services to riders in their area. The entire process from connecting with riders to receiving payments can be managed through a smartphone application.

To start earning as a ride-sharing driver you need to meet certain requirements like having a valid driver's license a clean driving record and a registered vehicle. Once you fulfill these prerequisites you can sign up with a ride-sharing service and complete their onboarding process which includes background checks and verification of your documents.

After becoming a ride-sharing driver you can set your own availability and start accepting ride requests through the app. The app provides you with all the necessary information about the rider including the pickup and drop-off locations. The payment for each ride is also managed through the app making it convenient for both the driver and the passenger.

Earnings in the ride-sharing sector depend on multiple factors such as the number of rides completed driving during peak hours or special events and the distance traveled. It is crucial to consider the costs associated with maintaining your vehicle such as fuel and maintenance to ensure you are earning a profit.

2. Food Delivery: Expanding Your Earnings Potential

Food delivery services such as DoorDash Grubhub and Uber Eats have become incredibly popular as people increasingly rely on the convenience of having food delivered to their homes or offices. These platforms connect drivers with restaurants and customers allowing them to earn money by delivering meals.

Becoming a food delivery driver requires similar prerequisites as ride-sharing services including a driver's license and a registered vehicle. However some food delivery platforms also offer the option to deliver food using a bicycle or a scooter providing more flexibility in transportation methods.

To start earning you need to sign up as a driver with a food delivery platform and complete their onboarding process. This typically includes providing your personal information vehicle details (if applicable and completing any necessary background checks.

Once approved you can start accepting delivery requests through the app. The app provides you with information about the order restaurant location and customer address. The payment for each delivery is usually a combination of a base fee a per-mile fee and tips. Just like ride-sharing you have the freedom to choose your availability and can work whenever it fits your schedule.

Food delivery can be a lucrative gig especially during peak meal times weekends and holidays. It is important to be efficient in managing your deliveries to maximize your earnings. Developing strong navigation and time management skills will help you complete deliveries promptly and serve more customers.

3. Task-Based Gig Platforms: Completing Jobs on Demand

Task-based gig platforms like TaskRabbit Fiverr and Upwork offer a wide range of opportunities to complete tasks or projects for clients. These platforms provide a platform for individuals with various skills to offer their services to people in need. From virtual assistance to graphic design writing or even running errands there is a wide variety of tasks available.

To get started you need to create a profile on the desired task-based gig platform. This profile acts as your resume and showcases your skills and experience. Clients can browse through profiles and hire individuals based on their requirements.

Once you have secured a job the communication and completion of tasks are usually managed through the platform's messaging system. Some platforms also offer built-in payment systems that allow you to receive payment directly.

The earnings in task-based gig platforms vary greatly depending on the nature of the task and your level of expertise. You can set your own rates for the tasks you offer but it is important to consider factors like competition market demand and the complexity of the task when determining your pricing.

Building a positive reputation by delivering high-quality work and providing excellent customer service is essential to attracting more clients and earning a steady income on these platforms. As you gain experience and develop your skills you may be able to secure higher-paying and more complex tasks.

4. Home Rental Services: Generating Extra Income

Home rental services like Airbnb and Vrbo have opened up a new avenue for individuals to earn money by renting out spare rooms apartments or even entire homes. These platforms allow hosts to list their properties and connect with travelers who are looking for accommodation.

To become a host you need to create a listing on the platform which includes providing detailed information about your property setting pricing and uploading attractive photos. It is important to highlight the unique features and amenities of your property to attract potential guests.

The smartphone application provided by these platforms allows hosts to manage their listings and handle bookings. It provides a user-friendly interface to communicate with guests accept or decline booking requests and manage all aspects of the rental process.

Earnings in the home rental sector depend on various factors including location property size demand and the quality of the listing. Hosts can set their own nightly rates and adjust them based on demand and availability. Additionally hosts may charge additional fees for cleaning or extra services.

Being a successful host requires attention to detail and excellent hospitality skills. Providing a clean and comfortable space being responsive to guest inquiries and creating a welcoming and enjoyable experience can help you attract positive reviews and repeat bookings.

Conclusion:

The gig economy has revolutionized the way people earn income providing them with flexible opportunities to work on their own terms. With the advent of smartphones participating in the gig economy has become even more accessible and convenient.

In this chapter we explored four popular gig economy sectors where individuals can earn money using their smartphones: ride-sharing services food delivery task-based gig platforms and home rental services. Each sector offers unique opportunities for individuals to earn income based on their skills resources and availability.

Whether you choose to become a ride-sharing driver a food delivery person a freelancer offering services on task-based platforms or a host renting out your property the gig economy presents a range of options for individuals looking to supplement their income or establish a full-time gig.

However it is important to approach these opportunities with careful consideration. Factors such as expenses competition market demand and the level of effort required should be taken into account when deciding on your gig economy pursuits.

By leveraging the power of smartphones and the gig economy individuals can create new streams of income gain flexibility in their work-life balance and even turn their gig into a successful full-time career. The key is to identify the right opportunities invest time and effort and provide exceptional service to clients or customers.

50 ways to earn money using a mobile device

1. Online surveys: You can sign up for survey platforms such as Swagbucks or Survey Junkie to complete online surveys and earn cash or gift cards.

2. Microtask apps: Apps like Amazon Mechanical Turk or Clickworker allow you to perform small tasks for pay such as data entry or image tagging.

3. Gig platforms: Join gig platforms like Fiverr or TaskRabbit and offer your skills or services to clients such as graphic design writing or virtual assistance.

4. Freelance writing: Write articles blog posts or website content on platforms like Upwork or Freelancer for clients and get paid for your writing skills.

5. Transcription: Use mobile apps like TranscribeMe or GoTranscript to transcribe audio or video files and earn money.

6. Language tutoring: Offer language tutoring services through apps like Cambly or iTalki where you can connect with people who want to learn your native language.

7. Virtual assistance: Provide virtual assistance to individuals or businesses using freelance platforms like Upwork or remote job boards like VirtualAssistantJobs.com.

8. Data entry: Utilize mobile apps or websites that offer data entry tasks such as Amazon Mechanical Turk or Clickworker.

9. App testing: Sign up to be a beta tester for mobile apps or participate in user testing to identify any bugs or usability issues. Platforms like UserTesting or Testbirds offer payment for such tasks.

10. Online tutoring: Use mobile tutoring apps like Chegg Tutors or Tutor.com to teach subjects like math science or languages to students.

11. Social media management: Offer social media management services for businesses and individuals helping them grow their online presence and engagement.

12. Stock photography: Sell your photos online through platforms like Shutterstock or iStock earning royalties each time someone purchases your images.

13. Mobile gaming: Play mobile games that offer rewards or real cash prizes by participating in tournaments or completing tasks within the games.

14. eBook publishing: Write and publish your own eBooks on platforms like Amazon Kindle Direct Publishing earning royalties for each book sold.

15. Content creation: Create and upload videos or live streams on platforms like YouTube or Twitch monetizing your content through ads sponsorships or donations.

16. Affiliate marketing: Promote products or services through your mobile device by joining affiliate programs and earning commissions for every sale made through your referral.

17. Podcasting: Start a podcast on a topic of interest and monetize it through sponsorships advertisements or donations from your listeners.

18. Online coaching or consulting: Offer your expertise in a specific field such as fitness personal finance or career advice through coaching or consulting services.

19. Instagram influencer: Build a following on Instagram by sharing engaging content and collaborating with brands for sponsored posts or brand partnerships.

20. App development: Develop your own mobile apps or offer app development services to clients earning income from app sales or development fees.

21. Mystery shopping: Use mobile apps like Mobee or Field Agent to complete mystery shopping tasks and provide feedback on retail experiences.

22. Voiceover work: Use your mobile device to record and submit voiceover samples for commercials audiobooks or podcasts on platforms like Voices.com or Fiverr.

23. Online fundraising: Utilize mobile crowdfunding platforms like Kickstarter or GoFundMe to raise money for personal projects or causes.

24. Social media marketing: Offer social media marketing services to businesses helping them create engaging content manage their accounts and grow their audience.

25. Influencer marketing: Become an influencer on platforms like TikTok or Snapchat partnering with brands for sponsored content or product promotions.

26. Online coaching: Share your skills or knowledge in areas like fitness cooking art or music through online coaching sessions or courses.

27. Stock trading or investing: Use mobile trading platforms like Robinhood or eToro to buy and sell stocks cryptocurrencies or other investment options.

28. Sell homemade products: Use mobile apps like Etsy or eBay to sell handmade crafts jewelry or other unique items you create.

29. Language translation: Offer translation services for documents websites or conversations in multiple languages using mobile translation apps or freelance platforms.

30. Virtual event hosting: Organize and host virtual events such as webinars or workshops on topics you're knowledgeable in charging admission or selling recordings.

31. Rent out your belongings: Use mobile apps like Airbnb or Turo to rent out your spare bedroom car or other possessions to earn extra money.

32. Mobile advertising: Join mobile ad networks like AdMob or InMobi to display ads within your own mobile apps or on your website earning revenue from ad impressions or clicks.

33. Online bookkeeping: Provide remote bookkeeping services using mobile accounting apps like QuickBooks or FreshBooks helping businesses manage their finances.

34. Website testing: Test and review websites for usability functionality and user experience through platforms like Userlytics or Userfeel.

35. Online data analysis: Analyze data and provide insights to businesses through platforms like Upwork or Freelancer using data analysis software or tools.

36. Rent out office space: Use mobile apps like Breather or LiquidSpace to rent out your unused office space to freelancers or small businesses.

37. Remote graphic design: Offer graphic design services using mobile design apps like Canva or Adobe Photoshop creating logos branding materials or social media graphics.

38. Online music lessons: Teach music lessons through mobile apps like Yousician or Smule connecting with students who want to learn various instruments or improve their singing skills.

39. Web development: Build and design websites for individuals or businesses using mobile-friendly website building apps or coding platforms.

40. Online focus groups: Participate in online focus groups through platforms like Toluna or Vindale Research providing feedback or opinions on various products or services.

41. Remote customer support: Offer customer support services to businesses through live online chat or phone support using mobile communication apps or platforms.

42. Language transcription: Transcribe documents meetings or interviews in different languages using mobile translation apps or transcription software.

43. Online research: Conduct online research for individuals or businesses on specific topics or industries providing them with valuable information or insights.

44. Ghostwriting: Write books articles or blog posts on behalf of clients who may not have the time or writing skills using mobile writing apps or platforms.

45. Teach online courses: Create and sell online courses on platforms like Udemy or Teachable sharing your expertise in various subjects or skills.

46. Mobile game development: Develop and publish your own mobile games on platforms like the App Store or Google Play earning revenue from in-app purchases or ads.

47. User interface design: Design user-friendly interfaces for mobile apps or websites using mobile design apps or software.

48. Online data entry: Offer remote data entry services to businesses or individuals organizing or inputting data using mobile apps or software.

49. Social media advertising: Create and manage social media ad campaigns for businesses helping them reach their target audience and generate leads or sales.

50. Mobile affiliate marketing: Promote mobile apps games or other mobile products through affiliate programs earning commissions for every download or purchase made through your referral link.

These are just a few mobile-based ways to earn money but remember that the earning potential may vary based on your skills efforts and the opportunities available in your region.

50 tips to help you use your smartphone exclusively for work purposes

1. Separate work and personal apps: Create separate folders or screens for work-related apps to minimize distractions.

2. Disable social media notifications: Turn off notifications for social media apps to avoid interruptions during work hours.

3. Use productivity apps: Explore productivity apps like task managers calendars and note-taking apps to stay organized and focused.

4. Create a dedicated work email account: Set up a separate email account specifically for work-related communication.

5. Enable email filters: Set up filters to prioritize work-related emails and categorize them accordingly.

6. Utilize cloud storage: Save important work documents and files to a cloud storage service for easy and secure access.

7. Utilize collaboration tools: Install collaboration tools like Google Drive Dropbox or Microsoft Teams to collaborate with colleagues efficiently.

8. Enable two-factor authentication: Protect your work-related apps and accounts by enabling two-factor authentication for added security.

9. Set up a professional voicemail: Customize your voicemail

message to reflect professionalism and provide relevant information.

10. Use a secure lock screen: Set up a strong PIN password or biometric lock to secure your device from unauthorized access.

11. Enable work profiles: If available use work profile features provided by your smartphone's operating system to separate work and personal apps completely.

12. Utilize Bluetooth devices: Use Bluetooth keyboards or headsets to enhance productivity while working on your smartphone.

13. Disable non-essential notifications: Turn off unnecessary notifications from non-work related apps to minimize distractions.

14. Customize sound profiles: Configure different sound profiles for work-related notifications to easily differentiate them from personal ones.

15. Set work boundaries: Define specific hours for work-related activities and avoid using your smartphone for work outside those hours.

16. Use mobile versions of professional software: Many professional software applications have mobile versions that can be utilized for work on the go.

17. Enable screen time limits: Set screen time limits and reminders to prevent excessive use of your smartphone during work hours.

18. Utilize digital signatures: Install applications that allow you to sign documents electronically to eliminate the need for printing and scanning.

19. Use a VPN: When working remotely or accessing sensitive information use a virtual private network (VPN) for added security.

20. Disable auto-sync for personal apps: Turn off auto-sync for personal apps to avoid distracting updates during work hours.

21. Turn on device encryption: Enable device encryption to protect your work-related data in case your smartphone is lost or stolen.

22. Utilize mobile video conferencing apps: Install video conferencing apps like Zoom or Microsoft Teams to seamlessly attend virtual meetings.

23. Set up email auto-responses: Create auto-response messages to inform others about your availability or temporary unavailability.

24. Use a task manager: Opt for a task manager app that allows you to create and prioritize work-related tasks efficiently.

25. Enable app-specific passcodes: Set up passcodes or finger-prints for specific work-related apps to prevent unauthorized access.

26. Utilize productivity shortcuts: Take advantage of pro-ductivity shortcuts available on your smartphone's operating system to save time.

27. Keep work-related contacts organized: Create a separate contact group for work-related contacts to quickly find and reach out to them.

28. Utilize offline mode: When not requiring internet access switch your phone to airplane mode or offline mode to minimize distractions.

29. Utilize voice dictation: Use voice-to-text features to quickly compose work-related emails or take notes without the need for typing.

30. Disable auto-play for videos: Prevent videos from auto-matically playing to avoid distractions while using work-related

apps.

31. Manage app permissions: Review and manage app permissions to ensure work-related apps access only required information.

32. Disable personal hotspot: Avoid the temptation to use your smartphone's personal hotspot for non-work-related purposes.

33. Enable scheduled do not disturb mode: Schedule specific time periods when your smartphone automatically enters do not disturb mode to focus on work.

34. Utilize cloud-based project management tools: Use cloud-based project management tools to stay on top of collaborative projects and deadlines.

35. Utilize mobile expense tracking apps: Install expense tracking apps to conveniently manage work-related expenses on the go.

36. Set up default calendar alerts: Configure default calendar alerts to remind you about upcoming work-related events or meetings.

37. Utilize offline reading apps: Install apps like Pocket or Instapaper to save work-related articles and read them offline during commute or downtime.

38. Enable face recognition or fingerprint unlock: Use biometric authentication methods to quickly unlock your phone for work-related activities.

39. Set up contact groups: Create contact groups for work-related purposes such as team members or clients to easily manage and communicate with them.

40. Utilize personal hotspot for work devices: If needed use your smartphone's personal hotspot feature to connect work devices like laptops or tablets.

41. Enable app-specific notifications: Customize the notifica-

tion settings for work-related apps to ensure important updates are not missed.

42. Utilize mobile CRM tools: If your work involves customer relationship management (CRM install mobile CRM apps for on-the-go access.

43. Use mobile scanning apps: Install scanning apps to easily convert physical documents into digital files for work-related purposes.

44. Utilize mobile accounting apps: If you handle work-related finances install accounting apps to manage invoices expenses and receipts.

45. Utilize mobile project tracking apps: Install project tracking apps to monitor progress timelines and tasks associated with work projects.

46. Utilize mobile time tracking apps: Install time tracking apps to accurately record and manage work-related hours and activities.

47. Prioritize app updates: Ensure work-related apps are always updated to benefit from the latest features improvements and security patches.

48. Utilize mobile CRM tools: If your work involves customer relationship management (CRM install mobile CRM apps for on-the-go access.

49. Minimize social media usage: Restrict social media usage on your smartphone during work hours to maintain focus and productivity.

50. Implement a digital detox: Take periodic breaks from your smartphone by utilizing features like screen time limits or engaging in activities that do not require smartphone usage.

Remember these tips are intended to help you maintain a work-focused approach while using your smartphone. It's essential to strike a balance and prioritize your mental well-being by taking regular breaks and managing your screen time effectively.